Mary grew up in Erie, PA, where she met her husband of 25 years. They are both retired and now living in sunny South Carolina. She enjoys cooking, writing, piano, and guitar playing, as well as painting and singing. She has one daughter who is living with her husband and son in Colorado.

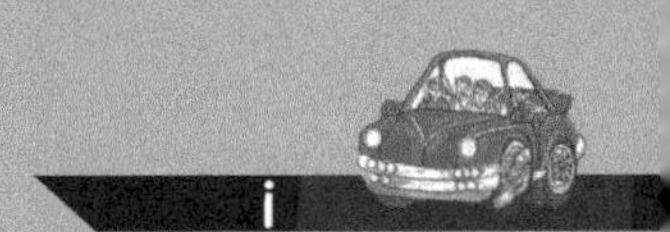

I WAS...

A RECYCLING BOOK FOR CHILDREN OF ALL AGES

MARY SCHMEISSER

Illustrated by Bobbie Hayes

AUSTIN MACAULEY PUBLISHERS™

LONDON • CAMBRIDGE • NEW YORK • SHARJAH

Ordering Information
Quantity sales: Special discounts are available on quantity purchases by corporations, associations, and others. For details contact the publisher at the address below.

Publisher's Cataloging-in-Publication data
Schmeisser, Mary
I Was...

ISBN 9798889106180 (Paperback)
ISBN 9798889106197 (Hardback)
ISBN 9798889106203 (ePub e-book)

Library of Congress Control Number: 2023918981

www.austinmacauley.com/us

First Published 2024
Austin Macauley Publishers LLC
40 Wall Street, 33rd Floor, Suite 3302
New York, NY 10005
USA

mail-usa@austinmacauley.com
+1 (646) 5125767

I'd like to dedicate this book to all the parents who show their children how to take care of our earth, because we only have this one, and a beautiful one it is. Most people know about recycling paper, plastic and metal but there's so much more to it. Get your children involved, as early as possible in local clean-up events. Show them through your actions how they can do their part to change your little corner of the world.

I'd like to acknowledge, and give thanks to, the many companies around the earth who separate our trash and find uses and re-uses for almost all of it. There are many dedicated individuals who are always trying to think up new identities for old junk, and for this, I am most grateful.

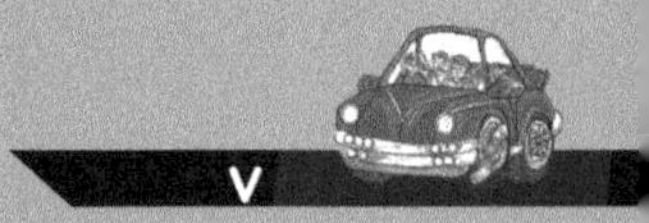

I WAS... THE WRITER'S HAIR.

It's true enough, I lay on her head,
Not blonde not black or even red.
Growing and growing.

It looked so fine;
My mamma washed it,

And boy, did it shine!

It got to the point, however,
Where I knew it was time I should sever
Its length from the rest of the locks

It was weighty like 70 rocks.
It was thick, you know, and heavy,
Imagine like a '62 Chevy.

OK, that's a bit overboard

So I had it cut off to the neck area.

Hid in a drawer for a number of years
I had hopes of making a wig.

I'd bring it out and show it off
But no one gave a fig.

Then I finally heard of a place
A place called "Locks of Love".
What they do is take your extra hair
And fashion it, so to speak.

Into a wig for a person
So their outlook isn't so bleak.
Some people lose their hair, you know
To many different ailments

So they're happy to get the real stuff
Even our old remnants.
I'd like to think that mine
Went to a waiting child

And she danced and danced
With her new hair
Like a bird out in the wild.

I Was a...Tire

I WAS JUST A TIRE, you know.
Three more of me hung on a car down low.

We helped the family shush around
Took them here and there around town.

My brother Ed, up front, right,
Began to look a terrible sight.
Looked downright worn,
Sadly thin,

Till the three of us said "Goodbye!" to him.

Sister Jan was next to go,

Hit some glass, and so...

A nail took out Harry,
And I was last;

It didn't take long,
And happened fast.

I wasn't sure what would happen,
When one day there was a very loud crash

Everyone above me was fine,
But I suffered a terrible gash.

I found myself in a hole,
Everywhere tires galore,

Skinny and fat, tall and short
And oh, so many more!

I must've dozed off for a while,
Cuz suddenly I was somewhere else!
Attached to a tugboat, out on the water,
I was helping push a Barge!

A bunch of other tugs were there,
With a lot more tires like me!
I not only had just one life,
But easily had at least THREE!
(OK, there were only two, but that didn't rhyme.
Besides, I was just keeping you on your toes...)

I Was a...Leaf

I WAS JUST A LEAF, you know.
There is a tree with five leaves left
Am I sad for the tree?
Totally, bereft!

Yes, dear readers.
I WAS A LEAF.
And the cold winter wind

Was the obvious thief.

I ended up in a pile with others
Uncles and aunts, sisters and brothers.
None of us seemed too awfully perturbed
Till feet came through us and really disturbed
Most of us.

A giant fork gathered us up, flinging us this way and that. I had to laugh at Aunt Josy. She was totally flat!

We all ended up under a bush
And winter, it came and it went.

We gave all we could to the earth
And by then, were totally spent.

We perked up a lot when one day
A girl put some plants between us
And day by day, the sun made them grow – the
rain, it helped as well.

But we all knew in our heart of hearts
That we were casting the spell.

You see, we lived our lives to the fullest
Saw seasons of green and red

And our journey was never-ending
Cuz we bloomed through the flower bed!

THE END